1835
THE
MARTHA'S VINEYARD
CAMP MEETING ASSOCIATION
TABERNACLE
ERECTED
1879

The Tabernacle is both the physical and spiritual center of the Campground.

OPEN
COTTAGE
MUSEUM
OPEN

The Cottage Museum is a "must stop" for visitors to the Campground.

The Lawton cottage at 70-71 Trinity Park might have been the first cottage built in the Campground.

THE
Kasers

Bishop Haven's cottage at 10 Clinton Avenue hosted President Grant in 1874.

The pink house at 25 Butler Avenue is one of the most photographed in the Campground.

The heart house is at 15 Trinity Park.

Five peaks are found on this house at
1 Bayliss Avenue.

Two brightly colored cottages are found in Forest Circle.

8 Vincent Park is one of the smaller cottages in the Campground.

16

These two cottages are found in Wesleyan Grove.

2 Tabernacle Avenue.

Cottages in Wesleyan Grove.

This cottage at 17 Trinity Park was the residence of J.W. Hoyt, the designer and builder of the Tabernacle.

The cottage at 24 Butler Avenue retains its original construction details.

Cottages on Trinity Park face the Tabernacle.

47 Trinity Park.

1865

This cottage is in Victorian Park.

NAUMKEAG AVENUE

The Corbin-Norton cottage on Ocean Avenue has been totally restored.

Dr. Tucker's cottage on Ocean Avenue.

Cottages along Ocean Avenue.